�֍ Trolling

Douglas Lawder

·Trolling·

Little, Brown
and Company

Boston/Toronto

T03/77

First Edition

Grateful acknowledgment is made to Robert Bly for permission to reprint the
poem "And What If after So Many Words" by César Vallejo, translation by
Robert Bly and Douglas Lawder. From *Neruda & Vallejo: Selected Poems,*
edited by Robert Bly and published by Beacon Press in 1971.

Library of Congress Cataloging in Publication Data

Lawder, Douglas.
　　Trolling.

　　I. Title.
PS3562.A863T7　　　811'.5'4　　　76-53816
ISBN 0-316-51661-9
ISBN 0-316-51660-0 pbk.

Published simultaneously in Canada
by Little, Brown & Company (Canada) Limited

Printed in the United States of America

For my children

:: Acknowledgments

I am grateful to the National Foundation for the Arts, to the Danforth Foundation, and Michigan State University's School of Arts and Letters for summer writing grants, as well as to the MacDowell Colony, without whose assistance many of these poems would not have been written.

Some of these poems were originally published in *Centennial Review, Chelsea Review, December, Descant, Lillabulero, Michigan Quarterly Review, The Nation, New York Quarterly, Northwest Review, Per/Se, Perspective, Poetry* (Chicago), *Poetry Northwest, Red Cedar Review, The Seventies, Southwest Review, Sumac, University of Tampa Poetry Review, Virginia Quarterly Review, Wascana Review, West Coast Review.*

∷ Contents

I ❖ Crossover

:: dead raccoons

in the morning they
are amazed
as when the lights
found them
in a well-meaning gesture
lifting a spidery and black paw
from the road
the quizzical smile a little drunk
from so much light in the head
the sudden blazing up
of a double sun

then struck
by knowing finally
they are not alone
in the dark
they thought they knew:
    the distant whining
engines of the night
the thin and drunken lurch
of flashlights and the white
cry of dogs that circle
their first few thoughts
of sleep

pebbles   grass   trees   stars
spin in an arc
all shouting something new
. . . to remember . . .

⚏ Driving Nonstop into the South

     We drove away from hard patches of snow in Ohio
and now with the top down and the engine
quiet as a jet we move along the flat thumb, Florida —
south through the darkness of the second morning.

     I ease the car into an orange grove
and we pull at the branches. Honey odor of blossoms.
The fruit drops into the car. Citrus stings
our northern senses.

     The others have fallen asleep
and the lime-green dash lights glow.
Wheels turn ticking off the miles
and when by pink through palm trees

     I see an alligator asleep on the warm road,
swerve, bump over his tail and wake
the others, they won't believe me
— make me stop driving.

     In the afternoon I wake from a dream of Captain Hook
and of the green beast who swallowed a clock.
Hot oranges, grapefruit roll in the back seat.
The ocean rolls under its skin of bright scales.

:: Keeping the Light Out

When lines went down we camped in the kitchen,
nailed blankets to the walls and doors;
Bedding down on the frozen floor
was cave dwelling: woodstove for heat and light;
Red things that flickered on the walls
were real shapes rampant every night.

The storm went on hissing, snow hungry
over windows upstairs, a dangerous country:
Toilet bowls cracking apart, banking snow
sifted through plaster and board and we heard
every night white shapes moving in overhead
and each day we sank deeper underground.

When neighbors broke in they found
us shy, suspicious, a small tribe
blinking, packed in the closed dark.
They told of a hot sun that burned for days,
how the land for miles was glazed
thick over lakes of snow outside.

Recalling the Sound of That Winter

By day the black sound of thunder
as snow avalanches slowly off the roof
and hysterical whiteness grinds against glass
darkening rooms downstairs.

Far off the floundering snow plow pumps
diesel smoke into white air.

By night we hear its blade strike black earth,
a sound of iron rung through thick water

to where we sit packed in silence
in the constant muffled piling up
of snow — its white insistent brilliance
that leaps off windows into lighted rooms.

Before Summer Comes

You know it's almost too much
the way so much yellow
gets into some spring evenings.

You talk quietly together
in a parked car
of things you didn't know

Before the blue skin of sky darkens,
the slamming of car doors
and lights leap out of living room windows.

∷ Hurricane Season

It was summer under the Dutch elm,
a giant that had all summer singing in it
— the small cicada saw working on its bulk

until we woke into a black morning
to violence that sheared
off upstairs shutters   when
some thing came down the chimney
and ashes floated through the dark downstairs;

Then the elm made a noise   a sigh
you'd never heard trees make before:
grunted   splintered and moaning slowly fell
full length across the road

and when we went out into yellow air,
to the blacktop cracked from the tree's fall,
piles of soft decay had spilled on the road;

All afternoon saws shrieked into the bulk
until the tree lay stacked in yellow piles
— the sky suddenly opening up!

:: Animal, Vegetable, Mineral

This body in the garden
brewing its warm juices,
the sweating flesh covered with welts
where the lust of insects
has sipped blood out,
a rage of pure blind energy
burning up with desire to grow:
Bean tendrils fasten their grip
on the fence tight as a baby's fist.
The body's hair in its heat coils
like vines. Nothing can stop
the innocent lettuce — a row
of green roses, each leaf
a small wave in a pool folding out
from the center of a hard seed
smaller than a child's tooth . . .
I rise up swatting the misted cloud
of insects. The sweat of salt
drips into a pool where the last
of the sun puts down its light
and like a cataract I catch the white
dead weight of the moon rising up
in the corner of the sky.

ᛝ The Field

Somewhere in the field
we have broken open a hornet's nest.
A cloud of them rises from the earth,
anger growing darker.
I feel the horse tighten
and step crabwise. Her summer
coat has mellowed from its sheen
to a thick mat. She knows the carcass,
a dead deer the hunter never found
tangled in barbed wire at the woods' edge:
She panics and won't go near.
A cold wind springs like a whip
and snaps leaves off
and she leaps in fear.
Growing islands of lather
whiten her thoroughbred's coat
and her white breath clouds
the field which is growing smaller
smaller.

✷ Summer's End, a Fever

The drowsy dog is chained, his eyes are yellow bees.
He watches as I rake and pile the leaves.
Small packs of yellow jackets growl, the smoke
like burning tea has stirred them up.
Two settle on my arm and put their poison in,
blond bodies humping sink in pins
so deep I have to crush them
first then pluck them off — a serum
sealed and working under skin.
The dog's asleep, a heavy shape that hardly breathes.
His body crushing poppies makes them bleed.
Up from town a chain saw's numbing drone
insinuates a thick honeyed sleep.
Warm air eddies upward, drunken,
filled with z's, with the heated scent
of apples and wild grape
that tilts the senses through
the long and reeling afternoon.

⋊ Sleeping the First Time
in a Bed Made of Old Barn Siding

All day whatever it is we are
is used up — water drawn from a well.
Then the thick dregs put the body
to another kind of test.

Like a hook on a long line
something has caught
and snagged on what is half-
buried in sand
under layers of sleep:

Suddenly awake from a puzzle of light
the moon going down puts through a knot
in the tall footboard. Standing over the bed

a strange horse that has come up from the fields
before dawn.

Falling back into sleep I hear
the well's pump underground
ticking on and off   on and off,
all its clear water rising

and under eyelids
the mare is grazing far out in the fields,
her ears that are ready to flick
for the first sounds down from the house,
the first pulse of life breaking,
the way daylight is overhead.

⠶ Air and Blood

Between us on the earth
and the sun it's an x-ray
— a few pieces of bone —
sockets joined by quicklight
drifting,

All the rest of him
a nimbus of light filling each
filament of feather   a halo
of arrows around bone   light
keeping him high
in the upper air,

But for the shadow
thrown down thick as a manta
cruising dark over fields,
preying over the land
hungry   anguished his cry
is a pin scratching
the sky's blue glass.

Coming down to earth he skates
at a cant through a tunnel of air,
light goes out from
the clicking rush of feathers,
the beak is snapping for blood.

Then the body and the shadow
are joined on the arching beast's back,
talons and wings together
finding the heart for a moment
forever.

≈ At Dusk, Passing a Farmhouse

First their red smell — tomatoes
blazing up from the garden along the road,
then lights in the barn suddenly come on
with a leap out to the lawn smooth
as a pond right up to the double sliding doors
and startle into color feathers of pigeons,
their red eyes high in the loft.
Headlights bound through the orchard thick
with apples and pears before the road bends
again into darkness and the folding of fall
around us for good

✱Animals Bearing the Sound Away

It used to be there was no night.
It lay waiting under the water.
— SOUTH AMERICAN INDIAN MYTHOLOGY

Fish are curled, unflicking in the deepest, still
reddening water. After holding in their milk-
rimmed eyes the moment with cold wonder
the horses go back to their grazing
and the solid thunck   thunck   thunck
of the baler carries away over the valley

And the girl's shadow detaching it-
self from mountain shade
calls to him mutely to come home
for the day. She walks over the cut
field smooth as the back of an unmoving river
but for the small stand of rye
that will yellow and fall
for hay against some other winter.

Now fish uncurl and flick out bolder
from under the shade of river trees
and the horses —
who've taken with them a sound
they had never heard a man make
before that pulsed and stopped
pulsed and stopped arching into the river
and splashed driving the cautious fish
unstirring from the sun —

have crossed over into the mountain's shadow
where night for the first time begins
when for the first time a sound a man makes
has defined the night's long tunnel of silence,

And the first stitch pinches her brow
with its shadow of wonder more cold
than water when the awkward shape
unnaturally asleep by the river
will not undouble itself   get up
and touch its hand to hers.

✻ Dearth

Through the hot rasp of insects,
their scatter of spent sparks,
this final ticking down — a dearth
of seconds piling up,
a spilth of seed in dry grass.

The last bright crack of sun splits
down the river's back
and its rich silt gathers
at the very end of summer.

For the last time
the torn scrap of a bird
zig-zags over the field:
loss   loss   loss,
a rusted bell tolling,
its slow slap of wings
sunk forever into the woods

:: Traces

Receiving and gathering traces in,
the barn rests like an ark on this hill:
Down from the farthest field
a crow or a hawk lights
on the cold wire fence,
sets off a shiver that runs
through all the barn's wooden ribs;
the final scrape of the swallow's wing
on the gutter, alfalfa with its last sigh
settling down high in the loft.

With just a knock,
ice — a film mirroring turning trees outside —
sinks without a trace in the tank. A draught of air
like a gasp
lifts and twists with a curl
seeds left on the barn's stone floor
— traces on the edge of turning
that take the breath off, take
the breath off cold from the lungs
for another beginning   all over
again

❊Bourn

Night doesn't come down now like a shot
— winter's rude slamming of the door —
but lingers in midsummer like a girl
wanting a kind of attention she can't define.
Though the woods behind the barn darken
day keeps its equivocal traces:
Neither the sun's heady brilliance
nor the grave dark but these small
splashes of half-light: a flashing
of fireflies, pocket of glowing mist,
the bright flute-song of nesting birds,
foxfire — a phosphorescence that sparks
against a shore where the other
and the other's shadow meet.

II :: Low Water

:: After the President's Departure

The crowd like those witnessing a terrible
accident refuses to leave — a drunk that won't
go home. Under tense lights the runway's
slick as lust   the helicopter's skin of oil shines.
Now the grooved parts move and mesh
grunting in the night   blades cutting blackness up
into equal parts   the smell of hot oil   an odor
of complicity thickening.

  The bircher from HUAC stays in the men's room
  looking for Patriotic Sailors or the college student
  who wants so desperately to hear his words and the girl
  with metallic hair is burning for the prod of any kind
  of power and the razor thin man gone as deliriously
  insane as a dog skulks like a pariah on the edge
  of the crowd's madness which begs him to seek
  his notorious destiny and the speedfreak
  whose last floorboard of reason has broken through
  is searching through the unclaimed luggage of the drowned.

Above the helicopter winks higher and higher
as if the fierce blazing lights alone
keep it in the air. They flash out hotly once
and disappear — gone — a dead star.

In Mexico

the people know where bands
of black horses run in the mountains

where Mayan bones lie with white pearls
and thick silver plate mixed in

these poor people still believe
there is some thing inside a rock

that their fortune will never change.

The Ranch Couple

All their stubborn ways
are dead-locked
up in that high country.

At night the deep, mean-tempered river
and the bear coming home stung
from stealing wild honey.

:: Disturbing the Peace

Vendors of car parts, salesmen of foam rubber tits
are making it home through their deathlace carbon.
They check in cold from the blue
Pennsylvania dark at the sign
of the MOTE spitting red all night,

where their surrogate wives, week-day widows
wait in the bar underground beating down lust
and age and their multiple Xeroxed days
with booze and a motel bed:

the figure and face the same that lies
on Sundays. Only what sells best next
will change
to add another wing to the swimming pool.

Then the crash of a car
door splinters the cold. Outside
a dumb show gyrating fight:
the cuff and gasp of man and wife both
scotched by fate.

Enraged they slip on the thick
scab of winter
where the red light of the law
comes to stain the ice
and we fumble in the cold
for proof of who we are.

⁑ Suburban Tract

Only a mild erotic dream during the week
but obsessive and growing to break
on weekends when lust is finally upon them:
The lawn has got to be cut!
All day they are drugged by blue fumes,
dazed in the sun and the numbing drone
of the mower like a big bee caught
and angered in a net.

She stands by the screen door the red
hands clutching a dishrag. Dirty water
rushes with a gasping suck from the sink.
The growl of the mower is making her nod
and doze. The machine swings again
into shade that eclipses hands and face
and she thinks of the vacuum cleaner's
need for more dirt and the bottles of beer
with their sweating necks standing up straight
in the Frigidaire.

On the bedside table the radio with its
smiling dials sits smug as a housecat
with its secret news and the clock
whose hands in an endless sweeping ring
are whispering, *come sleep   come sleep*.

⠶ What Happened at the Beginning of May

FOR K.

When she fell
she fell through
all of April.

Blue evenings
bruised her hips.

She lay for a long while
and when she got up
there was no face,
she had no face at all.

Blue, she cried blue
but love is what she meant.

What happened that she's locked
in April twilight?
We of sunny May whisper
outside her door.

⊞ The Double

It's the shadow   a
darker thing
gotten away at night
gone off on its own

when it's light
he calls for it
as if for an animal
he thought he owned
that has its purpose
it doesn't need to explain

and so when he casually climbs
the high tower of morning
with a deer rifle   the sights
checking out fine

he looks for a shape
to bring down   carry home
join up again with his own,
with what he knows for sure now
— ahh, the tiny bodies falling —
is lost for keeps.

⁂ The Man in the Cellar

who stores up hate
lives alone but with his family
collecting bones of small spring birds,
shells of summer insects
keeps his own nail parings   teeth   hair
vacuum tight in a jar.

There are pieces of hate
always in his pockets   shot
through his hair   sealed up
in his teeth   under his nails
and hate especially at night
in his shadow.

One day his gentle brother
for no reason   beside himself   brought down a log
hard on his brother's head and hated
himself whom he saw
bleeding on the ground.

✹ Bible Belt Daughters

All June long they breathe
the small seeds in
of plants carried on the air,
asleep in the warm loam
of the dark are safe
from deep summer.
When the soft pulp of August
gives way
they mount their bikes
ride through corn fields
wind up their
I don't care   don't care   don't care
slowly around each tire.

✹ Late Summer, Long Distance

The hour early on the lawn
the heat not yet a shrill saw sound
and the day not shaped into a Saturday plan
against a burning, climbing sun.

Then shards of ice ring in a shaded room
and a voice of red flowers blooming —
screams that stitch into late afternoon
and all night long sprinklers bead the lawn.

⠶ Mark Twain's River

Water rose shrinking
the narrow island so small
that another presence
was like waking in a dark room
screaming, *Who's there?*

Only when fog closed down
could the river loosen a few mild secrets
— things not yet quite dead
and certainly not alive —
companions to the fog.

And what if the loaves
filled with mercury floating
downstream made the river's
drowned things rise . . .

How ever to look into even shallow water
after the river's vault swings open,
bread and quicksilver touching carnage
and years of late-night mayhem begin to rise?

⁜ Waiting for the News

CAPE COD, SUMMER, '68

Newspapers land on the porch:
Every day the thump
of a dead thing drowned
in a sack   news
of a mad euphoria,
of deep sea divers lost
gone down too far to know
the right way back.
Trying to keep apart these
daily appalling stories
I dream over and over instead
of station wagons filled with
drowned babies   a tangle of
limp limbs browned from the sun
and blue from what the sea
had done to them.

At dawn we wait.
The sea is out, uneasy,
a distant thrumming:
Waves breaking into sheets
of white paper against the reef.
A child's voice sounds all the way down
from the bluff so close
it must be some mistake.
Even the click of a beach stone

carries for miles along the shore
where hundreds and hundreds
of starfish cling under the sky
loosened from the night
waiting   stranded   in low water.

✷ Waiting for the Wrecker —

where tracks laid down upon so much flatness
run right into the afternoon's horizon
a direction no one ever before has taken,

from out of where my son putting his head to the rails
hears the hard molecules' deep ringing
even as our eyes follow the tracks
and we see them joined in a distant tip
and still there is no train,

he shudders hearing that great weight
coming at us from out of the stranded morning
in the train's distant moment of passing

— waiting for the far red lights
that just now begin to flicker.

✷ For John H
Dead Suddenly of Cancer
Spring '75

That season slut spring
was up and about: wind
had its way with the mountain,
rain scored in the over-flowing river bed
and that jealous bitch
fell for you, caught you
without a stitch
as if in flagrante delicto
— which was only, merely
    your life.

Inside the marrow bone she tapped
back her report — the itch of cells breeding
until the first taut leaping up of nerves in your neck.

Then for a time we watched
as she diddled you,
limbs thinning
to arms of a broom.

Every day the innocent, hopeful O
around the mouth of your drinking glass
but on the last when you knocked it to the floor
the curved edge broke into a glassy grin.

She had you as sure
as water and wind,
as the proliferate flood
that creeps at night into town
— even as the mountain you had been.

⚙ Homesteader's Dream

the hard surface of his sleep feathered
by something undone   ticking in the wind
feathering his sleep with sound

which is colored by white stones on red clay
and by the indian who is thinking
of a white girl's pink fingernail

hooves click stones

the indian is erased
by the black woods close at hand/or
by what a sleeper will make of the wind.

✸Cave-In

An experienced miner claims to know by a
sort of instinct when the roof is unsafe; the
way he puts it is that he "can feel the weight
on him." He can, for instance, hear the faint
creaking of the props.

— GEORGE ORWELL, The Road to Wigan Pier

The black slab has lured
them down like lust.
Deep under the bed
their sky is chipped
into a million stars
and the constellations shift
as each one hunched
sweeps his lamp   his night eye
centered in the head
to move   rearrange
his own dark sky

that fails them all   the hands
that feel the first faint
trembling overhead,
the blood that runs
into fingertips
before the sob
and the mouths filling up
with planets   moons   stars

and brings above them
blind pit ponies
suddenly to their knees   small
moons rolling in their eyes   amazed
they kneel on a shuddering roof
where the bleached grass shakes,
starlight wobbles in a ditch.

The rift flows under a house,
trembles pins and needles
in a glass   a woman in her bed
first feels her blood
run to fingertips before
the deep underground cough
that knocks all light
from her looking glass
scattering like stars
on the floor.

❉ Dogfight before Dawn

Red the bulldog runs out into the night,
latches jaws on the neighbor's mean bitch.
They growl and snap in circles and tear
the throat with teeth and claws.
Dragging them over the wet lawn
(to knock their snouts with a stick
only makes their eyes go more red with hate)
you shoot them with water from a hose
so they fall panting apart.

The racket dies off above the trees.
The innocent in their sleep begin to fight
a threatening tide that pulls,
that drags them thrashing down
in a wet grasp of fur and teeth
— just below the first pink edge of dawn.

III ∷ Wave Back

⠿ Motorcycle Poem for C.

We swallow mouthfuls of groundfog
rolling its whiteness over the road.
Headlights, porch and houselights
come ringed in wavering halos
and when a phone rings from a farmhouse
its notes string out in the fog's
beading of lights. Cows stand
under the dripping trees
with their eyes following:
that-one's-not-to-be-trusted
and she who's behind me light
as mist has circled around me her trust
and yet is changing, changing
into someone I've never known
in this estrangement, the fog's
opening and closing around us
with the engine throbbing
beneath its low understatement
bearing us homeward into a place
we'll never have seen before,
one shadow of two following
behind through the fog
that will catch up with us both
tonight as if for the first time
together.

✹Under the Divide

At 10,500 ft.

SIX FOR SUE WHO WAS THERE.

1.

Circling the lake. Then back again to your brown tent.

2.

Constant as the glacier above us — even in high summer
        gathering the sun's light in.

3.

All night the splashing of waterfalls into the lake — its wet
        edge.

4.

I listen always for the lead horse's bell that tells me — even in
        sleep — how near, how far away grazing she is.

5.

Your eyes bluer than the blue jay's wing — chips off the lake
        — that beggar, looking for a hand-out!

6.

The pink of dawn is the color of the laketrouts' flesh we eat
        together every morning.

⌘ Smooth, Precipitous Places

On a morning
early
when the canyon was smooth with ice
and our old convertible slid to the edge
nosed down   plowed snow
and fractured ice
in the river below
they hauled us up
unhurt
with ropes.

That night at home
(you softly flushed
from whiskey and a hot bath)
our house dim
in the black valley
we watched the last of the sun
crackle on glazed peaks
before going into the dark

✻ First Fire

The woods' summer-mellowed heat
rushes with an upward gasp
and its orange flame licks
the hearth's mouth.

A flash of Cointreau
on the tongue and in our mouths' soft blackness
— held as bright as a low note from a cornet.

The flame's splash of shadow rising and falling
on your bed, against the window's glass
— first fire.

Outside, the weighted harvest moon
rolls over and ice tonight
will begin to show
its first small teeth on the lake.

⊠ Soliloquy Very Early in the Morning

FOR C.

When you're not here girl
I damn your hair right
down to the roots,
your small breasts
full of sweet tea.

Outside I hear a pear fall,
hay breathing in the barn
and dawn still
a long ways off.

∷ Nightwatch

Your black hair snapping in a whip
around the white coast of my shoulder
and the net of it around the eyes
and rain ticking out its own time
against the window.
How was it later when we looked
out it was another morning
and another kind of hunger
standing up that urged
to be fed?
But the lash of your hair again
whipping in a hot wetness —
a stroke of a kind that doubles
the knees and the ticking of rain
on the window went on and on
and we were doubled   in touch
but lost to the world,
to the difference even between
black and white or of any kind of dawn.

:: Eating Strawberries in the Dark

All night the blush and cooling,
the rush of making love again,
nightlight pouring its milk
across the bed
and later eating strawberries in the dark:
their red flesh so bright
they flash in the mouth
when with each bite the teeth
bisect one to its inside white star-
shape.

The moon going down pales
the room to a watery milk.
Only a slight flush in the sky.
Star-filled, love-bruised, moving apart,
we enter again the warm loam of sleep.

✸ Inside the Dream

I'd walked out to the shoreline curved
like a thick coin
with the sea gone all the way out
but for shallows where a dash
of small fish sharp as a fistful
of needles flashed down through
tidal water. But it was the rare
snail shell — caracol — I'd dreamt of all night
flung up on land ringing
from the gulf floor's weight of water
among the scree and sea shards the tide
had left: moon chips like a strewn dream,
the last day of March at 5AM
when the moon was shell
and lemon peel thin.

I found it beyond the bar
wavering under water   warping
like a yellow flame
and raised it dripping, a small idol
from the sea: convoluted, a compressed fugue,
enameled pink and yellow and ending
with a swirling flourish
at the tip.

⋈ Poem inside a Poem

FOR T.

Night beetles thumped against glass
and tried to get in: red candlesticks,
wine and the crushed red beasts,
their rattle of armor
on the plate, but first,
you said, a poem like a prayer
before dinner,
so we wrote for my daughter,

> . . . black sea tanks clang
> their heavy limbs on
> edges of the zinc pool.
> Red antennae investigate the air
> above listening to why they're
> where they are after coasting down
> 10 million years inside the same
> black case hearing the tide's
> scratch and draw of sand outside . . .

And outside the black light
lacquered your dark-green battered car
that crouched on the bluff for the kill,
that later crumpled you up, but
— mirabile dictu — alive in its broken shell,
the moon swinging bright as a scale
eased back awhile on the crush
of all that weight which listens under the sea.

✴ For A.

D. 1956

Her voice in the morning was deep water
as she urged her frightened mare
into small waves at low tide.

At noon she rode into high surf.
The smooth sea held them for a spell
before horse and girl dropped right through.

That night even her tamest ponies
tried to kill each other.

▪ Wave Back

There are days when everyone
looks like someone I know.
Out there, it's Kay Ellyard again for sure.
Two hours later and I see her
drinking coffee black in Sam's Dinette.

And tomorrow, next week
I'll see you
waiting in line at the movies
or driving by in a second hand car.
It's the fingerprint of another's self
I try on everyone I see
trying to make it fit.

Now you know who it is. Wave back.

✄ Talisman

*I've always said that poetry can't
become obsolete because it doesn't
have any use and only things that
are useful become obsolete.*

— DIANE WAKOSKI

Red stone, chunk
of toughened muscle shot
from the earth's hot core,
tiny clenched fist, small
polished heart from where
time first tightens and starts.

From under the glacier's weight
it rolled out down
the mountain's river,
chastened and smoothed
by the earth's sandy grit,
by the hot flush of your hand
touching it out of water.

Now it rings in the pocket,
against coins and keys,
against all the junk in this world!
It rings useless as song and as deep
as the earth's heart down
where there is no turning.

◖ The Couple(s)

The poem as novel

Small grapes of the morning like poetry,
cold water pulsing deep in the well,
a bag of bright nails in the yard,
the smell of cut wood wet in the sun,
the mild bite of pain put on everything
and everything still to be done
— when love's first sting buckles them to the ground.

The long melons of the afternoon like prose
and by the poolside the gin drinks and the sun,
the new car bright
as a jelly bean on the lawn,
a glaze of clean order put on everything
yet everything looking to be done
— when love has rubbed them smooth as a stone.

∷ The Stranger

Even the red neon from town glowing
through the snowy woods seems right.
As I step out the back porch the last
mantle of clouds lifts from
a new covering of snow on Sangre Mountain.
A final flake drops with a small hiss
into my cup of black coffee
and I wave back to a stranger
who's come out around the bend
of the white road.

:: Foothold

Down there what is turning dark are rocks,
trunks of trees with a thin snow,
a whiteness that won't take hold,
weeds stalking the fields' white paper . . .

And now the road black as a typewriter ribbon
climbs out of the last mountain village,
lights going out in the valley,
starlight and no moon;
Above the timberline snow
white as the inside of an eggshell
and these thick tracks holding their own
shadows for a spell
— something to go on at last.

** Mid-Way

Half-way up the mountain I stop,
seek in the ditch a song or color.
Water moves down from the top
seeping under the summer glacier,
a permanent part of the Rockies
that's always taking light in,
where water coils down like a spring.
Its light jerks in the ditch —
bright pieces of a broken pocket watch
winding down into the valley;
then a slow ticking through stones.
I come down slowly and shaken
and hearing the small splash
of a well gathering stars in.

☷ Trolling

Through the blue jelly of the eye
the ocean twists inland again.

Always out on the gulf in a half-busted skiff
even when rain lashes the water dark and waves
rear up to whack the old ribs of the boat
I troll waiting for a thick tug,
the thing to lean its weight against the line,
feeling the strength of it, the wit down below,
and begin to pull a dark dripping shape into sight;

Or bring up dead lines   head back to shore
drink out the night with wine
caught up in a slow-motion pitch
of long swells riding them into sleep
then into dreams of silver bass   halibut
and the red pompano that swim every night
in slow rainbow circles just under the bed.

:: Soundings

Working below the frost line
I'm off on another lead underground.
The furnace comes on with a gasp.
Light on my hand's flesh weakens
as power is sapped for the furnace's
lung to catch its hot breath again.
Outside the wind rises and flings
snow with a slight tinging carried
through boulders — what the glacier
left behind — fieldstone for foundations.
Upstairs a child shifts and with a sigh
turns in bed towards the night again.
Then all is stillness and quiet —
The tall maple so close at hand
I almost hear what its roots grasp
going down through the clay's wet
breathing, on all sides, breathing.

IV ❈ Footholds

∷ Night Talk

It was talk that had been held back
when rain came down in its first
quick scurry of drops on leaves
as sharp as the tap of a typewriter
going strong all night,
then rolling off the roof loosely
into a line of washed and rutted pebbles,
each one a note,
bright wet even in the dark
— then there should have been talk
that glows the more for the least light
loosened from the throat
instead of clothes
and the kindling lit that only smoldered
in the sodden fireplace
before going out in the night.

⊠ Falling Asleep under Storm Mountain

  The small house high
as it's safe to be in the Rockies:
Storm Mountain so close
across the valley miniature deer
browse under aspen
near enough to invite them over . . .

  It's been three days straight
high on poetry. I turn to the plum wine
to cushion the crash coming down.

  Dusk comes rolling its long shadow,
a wave of running water across the valley.
Ranch lights below tick on.
The rusty pump labors lightly
bringing up water that was crystals
three days ago above the timber line . . .

  Like a barometer
the blue wine drops in the bottle.

  Falling into sleep you can hear
the crack of sage
deer climbing past the window
to safer country through clouds
that open and close like a door
into another kind of night —
into thin air.

❊ Trying to Write Again

These nights going down into the cellar
there is the sound of the dying elm
— roots scratching cement for water.

These nights the lacy fish wake
from their dark tanks and bump
soft heads on walls of light.

It is night again and time to search
for light, for clear water.

❖ Green Tomatoes

I come down to the cellar
for this ritual, the harvest moon just
having touched its frost of light on my right shoulder.
Underground there are the bright bushes
of plants, the tropical fruit of green tomatoes
brought down here by my children
who've gathered handfuls from the garden,
ripped them out by the stems to string them
upside down and hanging from a terrace,
the bulbs banging together with a green
ringing, each a chance in their tight skins
for a poem against a hard-slanted stinging of snow
on the north wall's fortress of fieldstone.
They breathe their moist sweat still
from the garden which rises and mists
cellar windows with a glaze that keeps —
that backs in the dim underground light
which works like a seal for us all against winter.

:: The Nature of Forms

Liking the conceit
of a fish's skeletal backbone —
how it's like a fern print
etched flat in a bed of coal —
more can be said for the fern's arched
and green-ribbed grace
and how the bones of a fish hold
his compact flesh, help guide his thrust
as he twists over the surface of a lake
before both fish and fern
lie down in the swamp.

:: And What If after So Many Words,

the word itself doesn't survive!
And what if after so many wings of birds
the stopped bird doesn't survive!
It would be better then, really,
if it were all swallowed up, and let's end it.

To have been born only to live off our own death!
To raise ourselves from the heavens toward the earth
carried up by our own bad luck,
always watching for the moment to put out our darkness
with our shadow!
It would be better, frankly,
if it were all swallowed up, and the hell with it!

And what if after so much history, we succumb,
not to eternity,
but to these simple things, like being
at home, or starting to brood!
What if we discover later
all of a sudden, that we are living
to judge by the height of the stars
off a comb and off stains on a handkerchief!
It would be better, really,
if it were all swallowed up, right now!

They'll say that we have a lot
of grief in one eye, and a lot of grief
in the other also, and when they look
a lot of grief in both . . .
Well then! . . . Wonderful . . . then . . . Don't say a word!

CÉSAR VALLEJO
TRANSLATION BY ROBERT BLY, DOUGLAS LAWDER

∷ Final Examination for English 300B
Advanced Poetry Writing
(A Take-Home Final)

You may combine your answers
from several questions if you wish.

1. How is it possible for so much pure light to be
   with you in a moving train under a mountain
   at night?

2. Explain: To grace the public with a private passion.

3. What is the correct color
   for the sound of one
   intolerable, collective anger?

4. Why do the opposites of sodium &
   chloride unite through electricity
   to become our own shared salt?

5. What do these hard, polished stones
   have to do with her eyes at midnight?

Extra Credit (Worth 12½ pts.)

1. How many poems is it necessary to write to be a poet?
   1. 2,401?
   2. 1?
   3. 5?
   4. None?
   5. Other?
   Explain.

2. Which of the following is prose, which poetry?
   a) green grass
   b) green
   Explain.

✢ Tools

. . . the fellowship of the shovel . . .
— PHILIP LEVINE

The curious dormant nature of tools
becoming more than themselves in their quick
and singular way of performing:
Snowshoes making the body's weight a lie
over twenty foot drifts — web-footed
again I get to the river
where the fishing rod asleep in its limber
length jumps suddenly alive when the fish's strike
leaps right into my hands.

Idle on the back porch the shovel's
angle is to the point in its way
of getting under the surface. Through use
its handle is turning to harder wood
from layers of petrified sweat
and the bridle hangs stiff on a nail
saving the shape of the mare's head,
remembering a mouth.

Red and silver rainbow trout freeze
on the snow as the sun goes down and the hot-
tempered ax head caught in the tightening grip
of the cold finally gets its crack
at a tree limb. Later the castiron woodstove
gathers to itself all the heat it can handle.
Smoke rises up to the cold night's crisp stars,
impalpable almost as words
but which in their right use still have their way
of getting us through to the world
alive for a moment.